Louisiana
impressions
photography by Brian K. Miller

Right: The opportunity to dip-net for shad draws fishermen to Alligator Bayou near Baton Rouge. The bayou is rich with giant cypress trees, turtles, more than 250 bird species, white-tailed deer, and—of course—alligators. Day trips aboard the Alligator Queen allow visitors to explore the 13,000 acres of the Spanish Lake Basin, of which the Bayou is a part.

Title page: The official colors for Mardi Gras—purple, green, and gold—were chosen in 1872 by the King of Carnival, Rex. Purple represents justice, green stands for faith, and gold stands for power. Mardi Gras beads are as colorful as the revelry that surrounds the annual bash.
Photo by Marcie Cheatham

Front cover: One of the oldest towns in Louisiana, St. Francisville is also the site of some of the state's most intriguing plantations. The names roll off the tongue: Rosedown, The Myrtles, Butler Greenwood, The Cottage. These reminders of times past often have oak-lined lanes leading to their front doors; the houses are filled with silver doorknobs, formal parlors, and marble mantles.

Back cover: Bourbon Street, lined with jazz and Dixieland clubs, eclectic shops, and restaurants, attracts visitors from all over the world.

ISBN: 1-56037-373-3
Photographs © 2005 by Brian K. Miller
© 2005 Farcountry Press

For more information on our books write:
Farcountry Press, P.O. Box 5630, Helena, MT 59604;
call (800) 821-3874; or visit www.farcountrypress.com.

Created, produced, and designed in the United States.
Printed in China.

09 08 07 06 05   1 2 3 4 5

Above: These nesting brown pelicans were photographed on Queen Bess Island, located north of the Grand Isle in Barataria Bay. The brown pelican appears on Louisiana's flag and state seal. One of the state's nicknames is "The Pelican State," and the brown pelican is the state bird.

Left: Curlew Island is part of the Breton National Wildlife Refuge, which is the second-oldest refuge in the national wildlife system. The island supports significant seabird colonies, which this bird-watcher is capturing on videotape.

Above: A pecan orchard in northern Louisiana appears mysterious and eerie on a foggy fall morning. The 28,000 acres in Louisiana planted with pecan trees yield a crop valued at over $15 million.

Facing page: Take a trail in Kiroli Park in West Monroe and be prepared for surprises. You might see a covered bridge, happen upon an outdoor concert or ballet, or spot a landscaped garden bursting with seasonal color.

Above: Dragonflies are among the most ancient of living creatures. This jewel of the entomological world, alighting gently on a twig, displays its aerodynamic wings.

Left: Kisatchie National Forest is a vast wilderness of hardwood creek bottoms, sandstone bluffs, winding creeks, and sprawling evergreen woods of longleaf pines. Louisiana's only national forest, its 937 square miles spread across the state in such a way that it's no more than an hour's drive from any major population center.

Reddish exteriors, shuttered windows, and vibrant bougainvillea flowers are part of the ambience of New Orleans' French Quarter or Vieux Carré (Old Square). Some of the structures were built before the 1800s. If walls could talk, they'd tell of mystery, intrigue, and romance.

Open 24 hours a day, Café du Monde has been selling café au lait and beignets dusted with powdered sugar since 1862. Overlooking Jackson Square at Decatur Street, the café is also a great place for people watching. Photo by John Elk III

To some, the spidery Spanish moss hanging from trees, surrounded by floating duckweed, is a simple spring swamp scene at Lake Martin, near Breaux Bridge. There is little hint of the complex and important role these wetlands play in Louisiana's aquatic ecosystem.

The long, lobed toes of the purple gallinule enable it to stride across lily pads as easily as it can swim through the water at the 35,000-acre Lacassine National Wildlife Refuge southwest of Lake Arthur. Smaller than the American coot, the gallinule (facing page) feeds on mosquitoes, spiders, tadpoles, and insect larvae, as well as fruits and seeds.

In Baton Rouge, lights from the I-10 bridge reflect across the Mississippi River. Baton Rouge is French for "red stick," which is one of the names Native Americans used for the area, probably because of their practice of painting poles with blood to mark hunting territories.

Fluffy white cotton (above) is ready for picking in the Red River Valley, east of Mira, in the northwestern corner of Louisiana. Young cotton plants (facing page) flourish in a field near Epps, in northeastern Louisiana. Although cotton was introduced in 1718, it was not extensively grown in the state until 1793, following the invention of the cotton gin. This machine separated the cotton from the seeds and hull.

Cameron, in Cajun Country between Calcasieu Lake and the Gulf of Mexico in southwestern Louisiana, borders a section of the vast Sabine National Wildlife Refuge.

A successful fisherman shows off a black drum caught from a jetty near Cameron. Louisiana added a saltwater fishing license in 1983; it has provided additional funds for fishery management programs.

Above: In 1835, wealthy cotton planter Daniel Turnbull built Rosedown Plantation, near St. Francisville. Inspired by their honeymoon visit to formal European gardens, his wife transformed 28 acres of Louisiana wildness into a variety of seasonal colors. Today's visitors will see azaleas, camellias, herbs, shrubs, and trees, as well as statuary.

Facing page: Oak Alley, a Greek Revival beauty at Vacherie, was named for the live oaks planted in the early 1700s that form a quarter-mile archway from the Mississippi River to the house. Guides in period costumes offer daily tours of the mansion, which has been restored and decorated with period furniture.

Above, above left, and left: The American Rose Center is America's largest park dedicated to roses. Off I-20 just a few minutes west of Shreveport, the center offers visitors the chance to see thousands of glorious roses—more than 600 varieties on 42 acres—from April through October. "Demonstration beds" show visitors how to grow roses in home gardens.

Photos courtesy American Rose Society

Facing page: The showy flowers of the magnolia have come to symbolize the South's rich culture and mannerly charm. This blossom was photographed at the LSU campus in Baton Rouge.

Above: Fresh and saltwater marshes fill about 284,000 acres of Cameron Parish, Louisiana's largest. The parish, home to four wildlife refuges, occupies the southwestern corner of Louisiana on the Gulf of Mexico next to the Texas line. This part of the state is called "Louisiana's Outback."

Facing page: Kisatchie, Louisiana's only national forest, stretches over parts of seven parishes. This sportsman's paradise is a great place to explore. The creamy white of the water lily and the purplish blossoms of watershield are among its attractions.

Previous pages: Covington was founded in 1816 and served as the center for commerce along the North Shore until 1956, when the Causeway across Lake Pontchartrain was completed. This horse pasture north of the city is an example of the amenities that have made Covington a bedroom community for New Orleans.

Right: Azaleas offer a touch of color to the grand oak alley of The Oaks, a beautiful plantation in St. Francisville.

Below: In addition to Rosedown's oaks and gardens, Daniel Turnbull and his wife collected and displayed statues from their travels throughout Europe and other parts of the United States. This statue of Saint Francis of Assisi is an example.

Oil has always been subject to "boom-and-bust" cycles. Louisiana's oil industry began around the turn of the twentieth century, grew along with the popularity of the automobile, but "went bust" in the 1980s. Drillers continue to tap the great swath of oil that stretches from Texas to Alabama. Today, drilling takes place at off-shore rigs, such as the one in the Gulf of Mexico near Grand Isle (above), or at on-shore rigs, like this one in a cypress swamp near Sorrento (facing page).

Above: A flowering oak-leaf hydrangea graces the springtime landscape of the 3,366-acre Tunica Hills Wildlife Management Area near the town of Tunica. Not far from the Mississippi River and the Louisiana/Mississippi border, the area is noted for its ravines, bluffs, and hardwood forests. It is an ideal area for hiking, birding, and wildlife watching.

Right: The cypress-tupelo forest is one of the attractions at Bluebonnet Swamp Nature Center near Baton Rouge.

Above: Always an event to look forward to, Shreveport's Red River Revel Arts Festival is an eight-day street party that unfolds along the river each fall. Visitors will hear some of Louisiana's best music during the festival.

Facing page: As you can see, visitors will not want to miss Independence Day in Baton Rouge. Fireworks, launched from a barge on the Mississippi River, cap a day of celebration; the Louisiana state capitol lights up the left edge of the photograph.

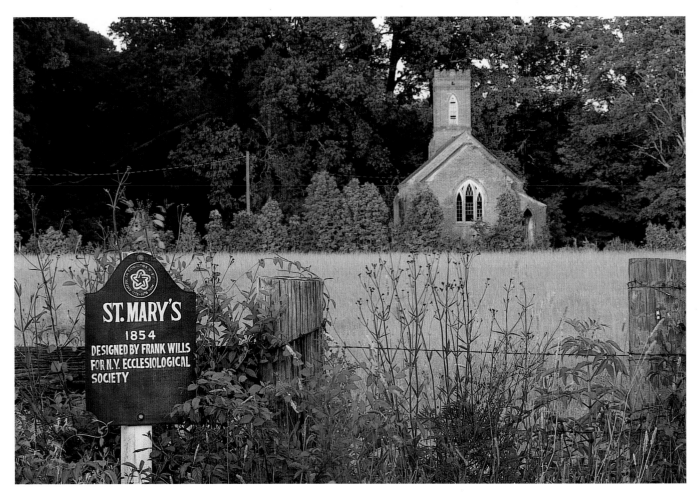

Above: The hauntingly beautiful St. Mary's Episcopal Church stands mostly abandoned and crumbling in a cow pasture near Weyanoke. Once a year, parishioners from Grace Episcopal in nearby St. Francisville hold services amid the ruins of St. Mary's.

Facing page: Rays of sunlight beam through smoke from an autumnal burn southwest of Cotton Valley in north-western Louisiana. A state of great contrasts, the cotton fields and farming in the northern part of the state are distinctly different from the bayous and commercial fishing in the southern portion.

At Sabine National Wildlife Refuge, an American alligator (above) rests near the shore. Baby 'gators hitch a ride on mom's tail (below). A large alligator (right) emerges from a swamp at Lake Martin, near Breaux Bridge. The king of the swamp and the state's official reptile, *Alligator mississippiensis* was almost hunted to extinction. Protection in the 1960s allowed 'gator populations to recover and by the mid-1970s, it was removed. Today, approximately 700,000 alligators inhabit Louisiana's wetlands.

Above: The moon brings a glow to the purplish hue of the twilight sky. The seasons bring great changes to Louisianans. The highest temperature recorded was 114°F at Plain Dealing in 1936; the all-time low recorded was minus 16°F in 1899 at Minden.

Right: The lights of the Triad Nitrogen chemical plant illuminate the landscape at Donaldsonville. Louisiana is one of the nation's leading chemical manufacturers.

The French Quarter brims with pretty pictures, no matter the season. Blossoms and greenery spill over balconies throughout the Quarter (facing page). At Decatur and St. Peter streets, a fall scene (above) includes foliage and a view of Jackson Square just across the street.

Left: Venice Marina is one of Louisiana's premier sportfishing spots. These waters around the mouth of the Mississippi lie only 75 miles south of New Orleans and offer the chance to catch marlin, tuna, snapper, shrimp, tarpon, and many other kinds of fish.

Below: Shrimp are so special to Louisiana that several festivals honor them. This shrimp boat, moored at Grand Isle on Barataria Bay, rests at sunset.

Framed by azaleas, the Louisiana state capitol in Baton Rouge (right) is the tallest state capitol in the country. Completed in March of 1932 during the depths of the Depression, it was a tribute to the tenacity of then-Gov. Huey P. Long. Ironically, Governor Long, who became a U.S. Senator, was assassinated in the hallway of the capitol, beside what is now the Speaker's Office on September 8, 1935. Monumental statues flank the entrance. To the east stands "The Patriots" (above), an armored soldier and the mourners of a warrior slain in battle.

Swamps help make Louisiana a sportsman's paradise. Camps, like this one west of Napoleonville at Attakapas Landing (above) on the edge of Lake Verret, provide hunters and anglers a place to tell tales about the day's adventures afield. Lake End Park on Lake Palourde (facing page), just north of Morgan City, offers the chance to see lots of cypress trees and, according to locals, "campground sites with more water around them than any other campground in the state."

Above: Louisiana is known throughout the country as a paradise for both game and nongame birds. The snow goose is only one of the resident species at Sabine National Wildlife Refuge. The refuge occupies the marshes between Calcasieu and Sabine lakes in southwestern Louisiana. It draws about 300,000 visitors each year because of its concentrations of ducks, geese, alligators, and a host of other wild things.

Facing page: Cameron Prairie National Wildlife Refuge attracts migratory birds to its freshwater marshes; a lucky visitor could see as many as 45,000 ducks and 10,000 geese. Established in 1988, the refuge is 25 miles southeast of Lake Charles.

Above: The Mississippi River was the water highway in the 1800s, and the workhorse was the steam-driven paddlewheeler. Visitors to New Orleans can relive the thrill of riding on a steamboat by climbing aboard *The Creole Queen*. Photo by John Elk III

Left: Most folks pay particular attention to the paddlewheel that makes the journey possible. Photo by Frank Aymami

Facing page: The spotlight on the *American Queen* docked at Baton Rouge adds a modern touch to the steamboat. The tourist industry has capitalized on river travel by offering rides that range from a few hours to several days.

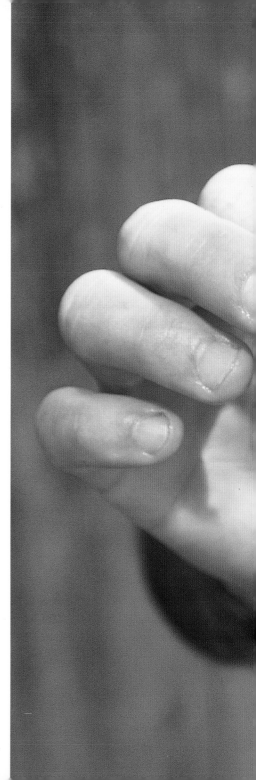

"Mudbugs," "crawdaddies," "crayfish," "crawfish"—call 'em what you will, they are delicious to eat and big business in Louisiana. Fish is often used as bait to lure unsuspecting crawfish into traps (above). Watch your fingers! Those pincers are loaded and fast (right). The crawfish is Louisiana's official state crustacean.

The great egret is a familiar sight to residents of southeastern Louisiana. This large, slender bird is conspicuous along canals and roadways in wetland areas. Egrets find Lake Martin (facing page) a perfect place for dinner—they skewer their prey (small fish, crayfish, mice, insects, lizards, frogs) with their long, sharp beaks. Two immature great egrets (above right) peer from their nest on Avery Island (home of the Tabasco hot pepper sauce factory). The great egret (above left) displays its splendid plumage in a portrait-like pose.

Louis Dronet has been playing the Cajun fiddle since he was 14; in 2004, the Cajun French Music Association named him "Best Fiddler." He plays with the very popular Kevin Naquin & the Ossun Playboys.

A family plies the waters of Alligator Bayou, south of Baton Rouge, for the catch of the day.

Shadowy cypress trees in a foggy swamp south of Breaux Bridge lend an air of mystery to the subtle colors of the landscape. Louisiana's intriguing features continue to inspire a wide variety of artists, writers, and photographers, who commit scenes such as this to canvas, print, or film.

Above: Preservation Hall was built on St. Peter Street in the French Quarter in 1750; it has served as a private residence, tavern, art gallery and, since 1961, a monument, operated by a nonprofit group, to authentic traditional Dixieland jazz. The music starts at 8:30, a set lasts about 30 minutes, and seating is limited—so come early. Photo by John Elk III

Left: The Old Coffee Pot, also on St. Peter, serves up delicious and inexpensive Creole fare. Try their traditional Creole breakfast—coffee with chicory and grits and grillades. Seating indoor or out in the courtyard—your choice.

Louisiana's swamps and bayous are havens for reptiles. Port Hudson Historic Site, southeast of St. Francisville, is home to this rough green snake (facing page). A red-eared slider (above) basks in the coastal marsh at Sabine National Wildlife Refuge in the southwestern part of the state. In the Kisatchie National Forest near the Fort Peck Military Reservation, a three-toed box turtle (right) tucked into its shell, goes eye-to-eye with a mosquito.

Fishing begins early in Louisiana. This young angler (above) is properly attired for a day of chasing fish at Chicot Lake State Park north of Ville Platte. He might know that the lake has yielded record catches of largemouth bass, crappie, bluegill, and red-ear sunfish. Chicot Lake State Park occupies 6,400 acres, with an adjacent 300-acre arboretum. The park also offers 22 miles of trails throughout the beech-magnolia forest, as well as the curving geometry of these flooded trees (left).

Lake Martin is a broad, shallow lake full of cypress trees; at one end is a thicket, which serves as a rookery for thousands of egrets and hundreds of roseate spoonbills (above). An anhinga (right), high in a cypress tree, dries its wings. The cypress serves as the anhinga's hunting blind—the bird spots a fish, spears it, flips it into the air, and then swallows it head-first.

Above: Colorful Mardi Gras masks adorn the walls of a shop in New Orleans. A tradition brought by the French, Mardi Gras, or "Fat Tuesday," is always celebrated 47 days before Easter Sunday.

Right: New England has its well-known boiled dinner. Louisiana's version is spicy mélange of boiled crawfish, onions, potatoes, mushrooms, green beans, corn and, of course, lots of garlic.

Sunsets over Louisiana are serene and beautiful. A late-August sun dips behind the trees that border Lake Martin near Breaux Bridge (left). Cypress trees frame a Caddo Lake sunset (above). Its rich history, beauty, and lunker-sized bass draw today's visitors to its shores, on the Louisiana/Texas border north of Shreveport.

ANCIENT MOUNDS TRAIL
POVERTY POINT EARTHWORKS
• • •
Poverty Point is a complex of
six mounds and six semi-circular
ridges built about 1500 BC.
The earthworks at this
site were the largest in the
Western Hemisphere at that
time. Many of the artifacts
found here show these Indians
had an extensive trade network.

Poverty Point Earthworks, just north of Epps, is one of the oldest and largest prehistoric settlements in North America. Built around 3,000 years ago, Mound A is the second largest Native American mound in the United States, measuring about 700 by 640 feet at its base and standing more than 70 feet high. The walkway leading up to Mound A (right) is an example of the self-guided and multimedia opportunities to assist visitors in learning about the people who built Poverty Point.

Weather and seasons take their toll but can also produce their own kind of beauty. A nineteenth century, weathered one-room Acadian Cabin (above) at Longfellow-Evangeline State Historic Site, north of St. Martinville, basks in the sun. A little farther north and west of the historic site, a nutria (left) snacks on grass at Lake Martin. A dilapidated shack in a cypress swamp (right) north of Gramercy shows its age.

About the photographer

Brian K. Miller earned a master's degree in wildlife ecology from the University of New Hampshire–Durham and has spent the last decade creating nature, wildlife, and travel images from around the world, including the United States, Canada, Russia, South America, Mongolia, China, and Southeast Asia. "I strive to capture the aesthetic beauty of the natural world and authentic moments in time," Brian says. "Through my photography, I use light, patterns, form, and personal vision in an attempt to create images that demonstrate balance and beauty."

Brian's photographs have appeared in numerous books, calendars, and magazines, including *National Wildlife, National Geographic Traveler, Natural History, Wildlife Conservation, BrownTrout,* and *Audubon.* His first book, *Birds of the Gulf Coast,* was published by Louisiana State University Press in 2001. Brian was a featured photographer in *Heart of a Nation: Writers and Photographers Inspired by the American Landscape,* published by the National Geographic Society.

An accomplished environmental scientist and wildlife biologist, Brian has a natural and instinctive feel for creating the right image for a variety of purposes.

Lake Fausse Point State Park is a wild, untamed section of southeastern Louisiana. Locals note that it's only 30 miles south of I-10, but "it feels like 1,000 miles from nowhere." Packed with wildlife preferring watery habitat, the remote swamp and bayou are best explored with the help of a guide. Catching the sun setting over Lake Fausse Point will make you toast the area's primeval beauty.